material pleasures

Lilian Coppock

Illustrated by Andrea Heath

First Published in 1995 by
BELAIR PUBLICATIONS LIMITED
P.O. Box 12, Twickenham, England, TW1 2QL

© 1995 Lilian Coppock
Series Editor Robyn Gordon
Designed by Richard Souper
Photography by Kelvin Freeman
Typesetting by Belair
Printed in Hong Kong through World Print Ltd
ISBN 0 947882 63 4

Acknowledgements

The Author and Publishers would like to thank the many children from Orleans Infant School, Twickenham, whose work has been photographed for this book.

They would also like to thank all the staff at Orleans Infant School for their ideas and support; and Elizabeth Allan (aged 7) for the cover artwork.

The Author would like to add a particular thank you to Faith Morgan for her enthusiastic help and contributions.

Contents

Introduction

Fabric can be used in imaginative and investigative work right across the curriculum, from Maths and Science to Humanities and Language. Textiles offer an inviting richness of colour, texture and pattern that paper does not do. Children cannot resist the softness of velvet, corduroy, fleece or fur, and they relish the unexpected magic of working with brightly coloured dyes. They enjoy handling, discussing and sorting fabrics, and many questions can be posed. Are the colours hot or cold? How many shades of one fabric can be found? Does the pattern have lines or curves? Is the fabric woven, knitted or bonded? How thick are the threads? What stitches have been used? How was the pattern made? Can the cloth be frayed, torn or cut? The list is endless.

Children need to be shown good examples of different techniques from around the world, and it is useful to build up a school collection of items for display, such as batik, screen-printing, block printing, dyeing, weaving and different types of embroidery.

It is essential to build up as large a collection of fabrics as possible for the children's own use. Jumble sales can provide old sheets, feathered hats or beaded waistcoats; the local greengrocer will supply vegetable netting; furnishing shops will usually donate out-of-date pattern books or lengths of unwanted fabric. Often, large stores will donate damaged felt or fabrics from window displays, and manufacturers of lace, buttons or beads can be approached directly for out-of-date sample books. Parents will gladly donate worn-out cotton sheets, old net curtains, odd balls of wool and candle ends for batik. Teachers' centres and scrap schemes also produce some useful materials.

Fabric is very versatile: it can be dyed, painted or printed; it can be gathered, folded, hung, stretched, wrapped, plaited, woven or decoratively stitched; and it can be made into many items such as bags, cushions, curtains, soft toys, puppets or clothes. Fabric does not have to be stitched - it can be glued, decorated, woven, collaged or used in 3D modelling.

Fabric work can be individual or collaborative, such as a quilt incorporating a piece of work from every child. Small pieces of work such as weaving or stitching make marvellous cards and calendars.

Many of the ideas in this book are adaptable according to the age of the child. Younger children are happiest with just a little stitching, together with gluing and decorating, and will need some adult help with cutting fabrics, threading needles and preparing looms. Children who are already familiar with a range of techniques will enjoy experimenting with mixed media, developing their creative stitching and mounting their own work.

I hope you and your children enjoy trying out the ideas in this book, and developing the techniques in your own way.

Lilian Coppock

SAFETY NOTE: Some of the activities in this book will need careful supervision by a responsible adult. For example, those activities involving the use of dyes, hot wax or a hot iron. Always cover your clothes, and remember to protect your ironing board and iron with newspaper when fixing colours on to fabric.

Dyeing

When using dyes, children need to be carefully supervised and well-covered with waterproof aprons. Painting dyes should be in non-spill containers and all work surfaces must be well-protected by newspapers. Wear rubber gloves when dipping, or use metal tongs. (*Deka L* or *Dylon* give excellent results with bright, clear colours, if you wish to use a commercial dye; and *Procion M* is good for colour fastness.)

Dyes work best on cotton cloth – old well-washed white cotton sheeting is ideal. Other materials give different results: the colours will be paler on man-made materials, and the colours will be different if the cloth is not white. A flannelette cotton gives a lovely soft colour-blending effect. White felt can be dyed in stripes or spots, or it can be wetted and dyed randomly, allowing the colours to merge together. Wools and threads can also be dyed in appropriate colours.

This book makes a distinction between painting dyes and dipping dyes, as follows:-

Painting Dyes are made with 1 teaspoon dye)
                          2 teaspoons salt) mix well and apply with a brush
                          1 jam jar hot water)

Dipping Dyes are made with 2 teaspoons dye)
                          2 teaspoons salt) mix well in a large container
                          1/2 litre hot water)

These dyes will keep for some time in sealed containers, for example, jam jars or empty paint buckets.

If you wish to use **natural dyes** you will need:
                          100gm of crushed fruit or cut-up vegetables
                          750ml of water
                          1 teaspoon mordant, to fix the colour (this may be alum
                          or vinegar)

Bring these ingredients to the boil and simmer for 20 minutes. Strain and cool. Immerse the cloth in the dye for at least 15 minutes, stirring regularly.

For
YELLOW: use onion skins, carrot tops, dandelion heads, saffron, dahlia, sunflower, camomile (use alum mordant)
ORANGE: turmeric (no mordant)
BROWN: coffee or teabags (alum mordant)
PINK: blackberry (alum mordant), cochineal (vinegar mordant)
PURPLE: elderberry (vinegar mordant)
DARK RED: bilberry (vinegar mordant)
BLUE-PURPLE: red cabbage (alum mordant)

Painted Flowers

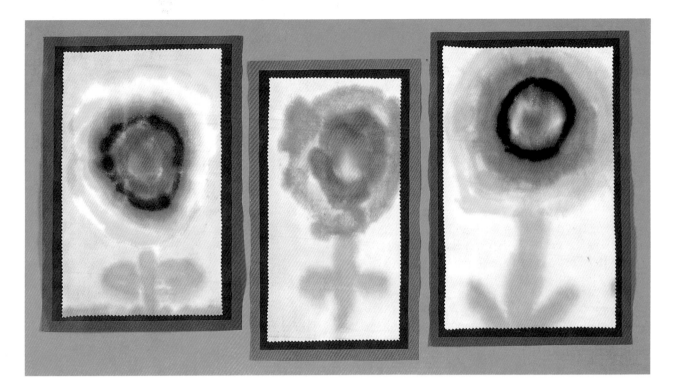

Materials:
Piece of cotton cloth
Painting dyes and large brushes
Method:
1. Put a spot of dye on to the cloth for the centre of the flower. Paint concentric circles around the centre, using plenty of dye and allowing the colours to bleed freely together.
2. Paint leaves, stems and a watery blue for the sky.
3. When dry, iron (through newspaper) and mount as desired.
Note: These flowers lend themselves well to further decoration with embroidery, beads, sequins, etc.

Butterflies

Materials:
Piece of white cotton cloth
Painting dyes
Scrap of black fur, pipe-cleaner
Method:
1. Fold the cloth in half and draw a wing outline lightly in pencil.
2. Paint dyes inside the outline, filling all the spaces. The dye will go through both thicknesses of cloth.
3. When dry, cut out the butterfly, and glue on a fur body and pipe-cleaner antennae.
Note: This method is useful for any work where a mirror-image or symmetry of pattern is required, for example, reflections in water.

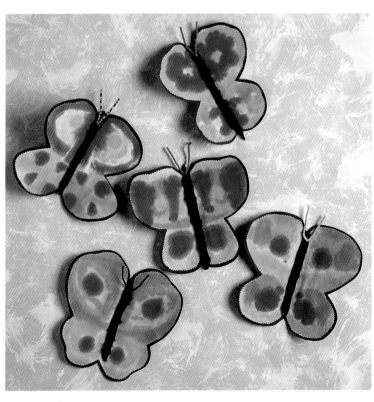

Egg Mobiles

Materials:
Piece of cotton cloth
Painting dyes
Egg template, black sugar paper frame

Method:
1. Draw the egg shape on the cloth, using the template.
2. Paint on bright patterns - spots, zig-zags, stripes, etc.
3. When dry, iron (through newspaper) and cut out.
4. Add an egg-shaped frame back and front, and hang up.

Note: Painted dyes are effective on mobiles as the colour is on both sides of the cloth. A frame is necessary to keep the cloth rigid. This idea makes a colourful Easter card mounted behind an oval frame.

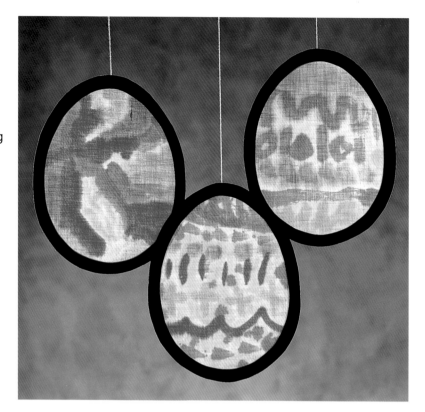

Autumn Leaves

Materials:
Oddments of white felt
Painting dyes - yellow, orange, light brown
Sycamore leaves, and brown hessian for background

Method:
1. Use a ball-point pen to draw around the leaves on to the felt.
2. Cut out the leaves, wet them and paint on the dyes with large brushes. Allow the colours to blend well.
3. When dry, sew the leaves on to the hessian to give a veined effect. Wool or braid can be glued or couched on for the stem.
4. The frame is decorated with sycamore seeds.

Abstract Designs

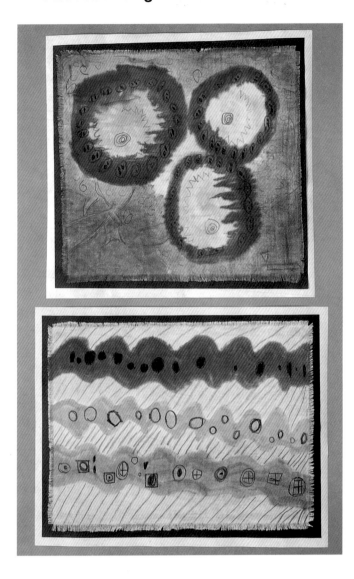

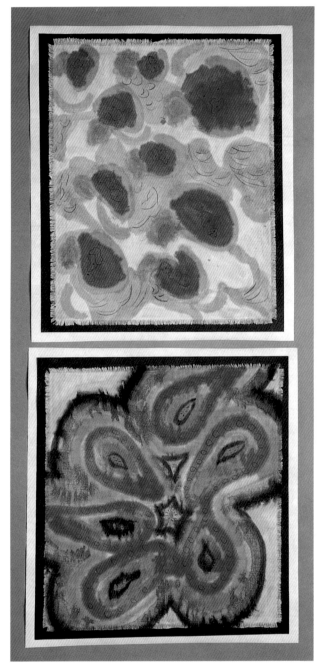

Materials:
Piece of cotton cloth
Painting dyes
Fabric crayons (optional)

Method:
1. Look at some examples of patterned fabrics and choose a theme for your design, for example, shells and fishes, flower and seed shapes, spirals, wavy lines, etc.
2. Plan it in outline on paper first, thinking about the whole pattern, and deciding where to repeat the shapes and motifs.
3. Paint on to the cloth with the dyes, using medium to large brushes, and allowing the colours to blend together.
4. When dry, further details can be added to the design, if desired, by drawing with fabric crayons.
5. Iron to fix the colours. (Remember to protect the ironing board with newspaper, and iron through newspaper.)

Note:
1. You may wish to experiment with fabric pens. Draw details directly on to the design, then iron to fix. If the cloth is wet, the colours mix and merge, giving a soft effect. If the cloth is dry, sharper patterns can be drawn.
2. Fluorescent fabric paints (for example, *Deka*) are also useful for adding special effects to a design.

Tie-Dye Chick

Materials:
Circle of white cotton
    towelling
Yellow dipping dye
Felt and cloth scraps

Method:
1. Pick up the circle of cloth in the centre, squeeze down the folds and tie elastic bands or string tightly in three or four places. This gives a pattern of concentric rings (see line drawing).
2. Dip the cloth in the dye for a few minutes.
3. When dry, remove the ties and iron flat.
4. Glue or sew on to a background, and add details of feet, beak, eyes and eggshells.

Note:
1. Towelling gives a good texture for fur and feathers.
2. Simple pieces of dyeing can be displayed as part of a topic on 'Shape' by putting a black border around each piece - square, triangular, circular, etc.

Embroidered Tie-Dye

Materials:
Piece of white cloth
Three colours of dipping dye
Decoration - sequins, glitter, lace
Fabric pens or glitter pens

Method:
1. Tie up the cloth as in chick example.
2. Dip one end in the first colour, the other end in the second colour, and the middle section in the third colour.
3. When dry, remove the ties and iron flat.
4. Following the pattern on the cloth, decorate with stitching, lace, sequins and stickwriter. (This idea makes a very effective flower head.)

Note: A similar concentric effect can be achieved by simply picking up the cloth in the centre and tying a tight knot in it.

Striped Tie-Dye

Materials:
Piece of white cotton cloth
Several colours of dipping dyes or painting dyes

Method:
1. Fold the cloth forwards and backwards in a concertina fan method.
2. Tie up the folded cloth tightly in several places, using string or elastic bands.
3. Dip each section of the cloth into a different coloured dye. Alternatively, paint each section with a brush, using plenty of dye.

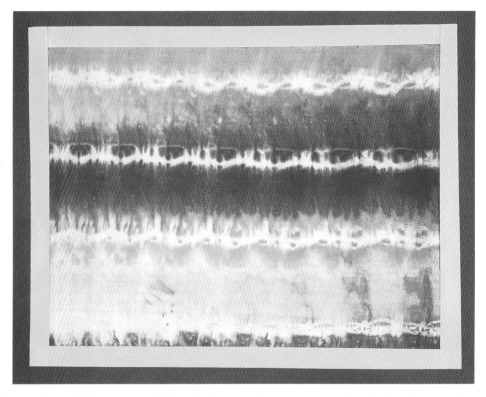

4. When dry, remove the ties and iron flat (over paper). The design may be embroidered or further decorated.

Note: This striped effect is very effective, when dyed in blues and greens, as a background for boats and underwater scenes. If dyed in yellow, red and orange, it gives a startling sunset sky on to which black felt silhouettes can be sewn.

Nigerian Tie-Dye

Materials:
Piece of cotton cloth
Dipping dye
10 beads or pebbles
Strong nylon thread or elastic bands

Method:
1. Use a pencil to rule five lines on the cloth. Mark the bead positions.
2. Sew small running stitches along the top, middle and bottom lines, leaving the ends loose.
3. Tie a bead as tightly as possible at each marked point.
4. Draw up the three lines of stitching tightly and fasten the ends securely.
5. Dip into the dye, untie when dry, and iron flat.

Note: All kinds of items can be tied into the cloth - conkers, peanuts, buttons, marbles, etc. Items could be tied centrally, with stitching around, or randomly.

Indian Laharia Tie-Dye

Materials:
Piece of thin cotton or muslin
Two colours of dipping dyes
Strong polyester thread

Method:
1. Fold the cloth zig-zag style, into four folds, then roll it from one corner, keeping an angle of 45°, until you have a long thin roll. Tie this up very tightly at intervals, wrapping the thread round and round to create areas of resist (see line drawings).
2. Dip into the first dye colour for a few minutes and allow to dry. Remove the bindings if you wish to use only one colour.
3. For a multi-colour effect, cut off some of the bindings and leave some in place. Re-bind in different places, then dip into the second dye colour, dry off and remove the bindings.

Note: Laharia tie-dye is traditionally used for turbans. A class project might be to join 30 pieces lengthways to make a turban length. Alternatively, the squares could be joined to make a stunning patchwork.

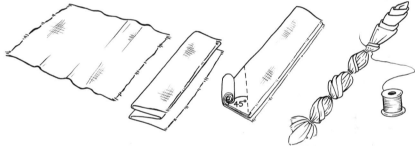

Faces

These follow the same principles as Nigerian tie-dye, using a mixture of stitching and tying. The eyes and noses markings were made with buttons and nuts tied up with elastic bands. The mouths were made with two rows of running stitches gathered tightly. Mark all the features on the cloth in pencil before you tie or stitch, then dye. These faces were stitched to a dyed background, and stuffed lightly. Further stitching may be added if desired.

Natural Dye Painting

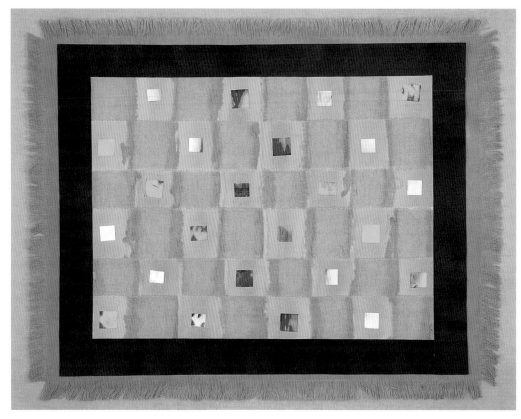

Materials:
Piece of white
  cotton cloth
Yellow-orange
  painting dye
  made with
  turmeric
Purple-blue painting
  dye made with
  red cabbage

Method:
1. Prepare the dyes, as on page 5. Use two teaspoons of turmeric powder to 200ml of water for the yellow.
2. Mark out the cloth with light pencil lines 3cm apart, top to bottom.
3. Paint alternate stripes of yellow and blue down the cloth, following the pencil lines.
4. When dry, tear the cloth sideways, across the stripes, into 3cm strips.
5. Reassemble by gluing the strips on to a backing cloth, so that alternate strips move 3cm sideways. This creates a woven effect.
6. Add stitching or decorative work as desired.

Salt and Dye

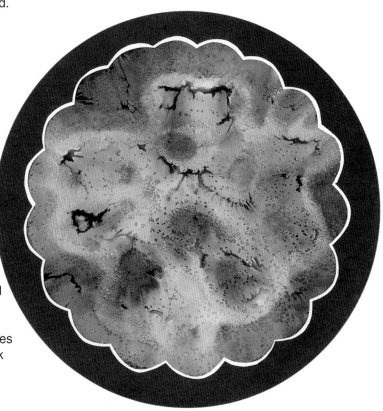

Materials:
Piece of silk
Three colours of silk paint or painting dyes
Sea salt crystals

Method:
1. Stretch the silk over a tin and secure with a rubber band or adhesive tape.
2. Paint using the three colours in circles, lines, etc., using plenty of colour.
3. Sprinkle large pinches of salt here and there, especially where the colours meet.
4. When dry, shake off the salt. This gives a wonderful 'stained glass' effect when used against a window.

Note: For the best effects, it is important to apply colour and salt quickly. The salt removes the colour, and forms attractive light and dark patterns.

Printing and Painting

African Geometric Design

Materials:
Piece of oatmeal coloured hessian, 60cm x 45cm, ready fringed
Fabric paints - primary colours, and black and white
White chalk

Method:

1. If possible, look at some African textiles incorporating zig-zags and geometric shapes, before beginning the design.

2. Lightly chalk lines on the hessian to make a 'frame' about 10cm from the edges. Then chalk the centre into sections using simple lines and shapes.
3. Mix the paints to make earthy colours and carefully paint over the chalk lines, adding further detail to the design as it develops.
4. When dry, iron on the reverse to fix.

Australian Aboriginal Figure

Materials: As above
Method:

1. Look at examples of Australian Aboriginal art based on the Dreamtime legends. Discuss the dots, circles and other patterns and look carefully at how people and animals are represented.
2. Sketch out a simple figure or animal on a large piece of paper. (The painting in the photograph is of 'Lightning Woman'. Turtles, snakes, fish, birds, etc. all make suitable subjects.)
3. Chalk the outline on to the hessian and paint in earthy colours. Patterns of dots can be made by dipping sticks into the paint and printing.
4. When dry, iron on the reverse to fix.

Screen Printed Friendship Quilt

Materials:
30 squares of sugar paper, 16cm x 16cm
30 squares of cotton cloth, 20cm x 20cm
A screen, taped and blocked off to leave a 16cm² window
Fabric paint or block paint (for example, *Colourcryl* fabric paint or *Secricol* textile printing ink)

Method:
1. Prepare the paper stencils. Fifteen children each draw and cut out a silhouette outline from their paper (not too small), discarding the border. Fifteen children each draw and cut out an outline window in the paper, discarding the centre. Half the prints will therefore be positive, and half negative.
2. Put a fabric square on a flat table, centralise the paper stencil on it, and lower the screen so that the window is exactly over the stencil.
3. Use a squeegee to spread the paint over the window evenly, with three or four pulls. Remove the screen and paper and let the fabric dry.
4. Repeat this process for all 30 stencils.
5. Cut the squares of cloth down to 17cm x 17cm and sew them together, alternating the positive and negative images, and using a 1cm seam. Wadding and backing may be stitched on if a padded effect is required. If you do not want to sew the squares together, they could be cut down to 16cm x 16cm with pinking shears, and glued to a backing cloth.
6. Bind the edges as desired.

Note: The theme for this quilt was 'My School'. Other ideas might be: my pet, my hand, my toy, a holiday memory, the alphabet, mathematical symbols, etc. Each child can contribute at his/her own level.

Polystyrene Block Printing

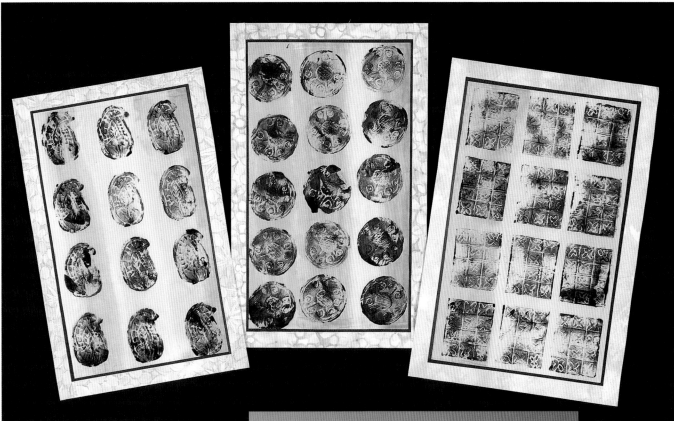

Materials:
Cotton fabric
Painting dyes, diluted
Black fabric paint or block paint
Inking sheet and roller
Smooth polystyrene tile

Method:
1. First make the printing block. Draw the chosen design firmly on to the polystyrene with a ball-point pen. Cut the block to shape and glue a card handle firmly to the back (see photograph to the right).
2. Dye the fabric by painting on stripes. Allow this to dry.
3. Ink up a roller on the inking sheet: it is important not to use too much paint - the roller needs to be audibly tacky. Apply the paint to the block and test the print on an oddment of cloth to check the paint application.
4. Apply rows of prints, inking the block lightly for every print.
5. When dry, iron on the reverse to fix.

Note: The designs used above are the Indian mango, the Chinese Qin tile, and a Nigerian alaro flower. Other round-the-world motifs tried out were the Egyptian lotus blossom and eye of Re, the Ashanti stool, Spanish rabbit, Peruvian cat, frog and bird, Canadian maple leaf and Celtic cross.

Marbled Curtains

Materials:
Marbling kit (for example *Pebeo* or similar)
Piece of white cotton cloth
Shoebox for the puppet theatre

Method:
1. Make up the gel as on the instructions in the kit.
2. Drop the chosen colours onto the gel with a pipette.
3. Draw through with a comb to create the desired effect, and take a print on the cloth.
4. When dry, cover with paper and iron to fix the colour. Cut in half to make two curtains.
5. Pink the edges and make a hem in running stitch along the top of the curtains.
6. Thread a string through the hem and hang the curtains at the front of the theatre, tying the string to split pins at the sides of the box.
7. The curtains may be opened, closed or tied back.

Making the Theatres
The theatres were made from children's shoeboxes. A slot was cut in the top for the 'scenery' - i.e. a drop-down piece of card, changeable according to scene. Slots were cut in the sides for the storybook character puppets. These were drawn on card and glued to lolly sticks. A decorated theatre name was glued to the top front, and a stage extension to the bottom front.

Note: Marbling on cloth is just the same as marbling on paper, with the added advantage that it can be stitched. An interesting piece of work can be made by decorating marbling, using the design on the cloth as a guide to where to stitch. Chains of beads can be sewn on in spirals or loops. Yarn can be couched into spirals, wavy lines or zig-zags, and small pieces of net, lace or ribbon can be stitched in with sequins and decorative threads.

Autumn Leaves

*(top left) White background, stitched print (top right) Dyed background, stitched print,
(front) Fabric background, sewing card*

Materials:
Fabric paint, in red, yellow and brown
Three inking trays and rollers
Fresh leaves
Pieces of plain cloth or card for printing onto
Painting dyes (yellow, orange, light brown) - if a dyed background is required

Method:
1. If you want to dye the background, do this first. Wet the cloth and paint on the three colours of dye, using large paintbrushes. Let this dry before printing.
2. Put a spoonful of paint on each inking tray, one for each colour.
3. Ink up the roller and roll it on the back of the leaf, from stem to tip, holding the stem as you roll. Allow the three colours to blend, and check that all the leaf is covered.
4. Place the leaf ink down on the background, put a piece of clean newspaper over it and roll firmly. Remove the leaf and let the print dry.
5. The leaf printed on card had holes pricked around it with a needle, with whipped running stitches through the holes. This was cut out and glued on a mottled fabric background.
6. The leaves printed on fabric may have running stitches added here and there along the lines of the veins.

Note: Pressed hawthorn leaves were glued to some borders. These can be preserved by brushing on some diluted PVA glue. This makes a lovely Christmas calendar. A striking border may also be made by gluing pasta to the card border and spraying it gold.

Fabric Crayon Design

Materials:
Fabric crayons
Piece of poly-cotton fabric
Decoration if required

Method:

1. Draw the design in pencil on a piece of thin, smooth paper. When you are pleased with the proportions, colour it in with fabric crayons.

2. Iron the design on to the fabric. The image will be reversed. The more heat you apply, the darker will the design be. (Remember to protect your ironing board with newspaper and, when ironing, press, lift and move the iron: don't slide it about or you will blur the print.)

3. The frame was made from border patterns ironed on to cloth and glued to a card frame.

Note: Unlike dyes, fabric crayons work best on man-made fabrics.

Fabric Crayons on Silk

Materials:
Piece of silk, and silk paints
Fabric crayons
Sequins, and small pieces of coloured foil
Tracing paper

Method:

1. Draw the letters of your name on tracing paper, in pencil.

2. Turn the paper over, draw round the outline with fabric crayons and fill in with pattern. Add a pattern around the name.

3. Iron the design on to a piece of silk.

4. Pin the silk to a wood or card frame so it does not touch the work surface, and paint on colours.

5. When dry, decorate with sequins, pieces of foil, glitter, or glitter pens.

Fabric Crayon Rubbing

Materials:
Fabric crayons
Piece of polyester/cotton
 cloth
Textured surfaces for
 rubbing

Method:
1. Decide what colours
 and textures you need
 for your picture. Rub the
 fabric crayons over thin
 paper placed on the
 chosen surfaces, using
 the side of the crayon.
2. Cut up the papers into
 the shapes you need to
 make the picture, and
 glue all these shapes on
 to a piece of plain
 paper. Further details
 may be drawn directly
 on the design (for
 example, a face).

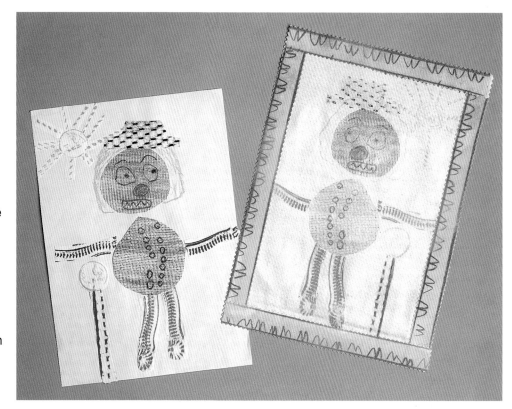

3. When the design is completed on paper, put the paper face down on the cloth and press with a hot iron.
4. The borders were drawn on paper strips with fabric crayons, ironed on to cloth and dyed with painting
 dyes. Pink the edges and glue into place.

Note: Surfaces suitable to try rubbing - plastic net and mesh, Binca, coins, rope, baskets, cogs, sequin
waste, embossed wallpaper, etc. Doiley sections make excellent butterfly wings or waves on the sea, or a
patterned dress. An embossed metal tray edging makes interesting curved sections.

Embroidered Printing

Materials:
Small piece of pale fabric
Fabric paints and sponges
Egg-box with flower-shaped base sections
Printing trays

Method:
1. Mix up the fabric paints in soft blue, pink,
 mauve, green, yellow and red.
2. Dilute a little of the pink, mauve and yellow,
 and put a spoonful of each on a printing
 tray. Use a different piece of sponge for
 each colour. Gently print all over the fabric,
 aiming for a muted background effect.
3. Separate the egg-box into sections, and
 apply undiluted fabric paint to the base,
 then print on to the fabric. Print a selection
 of coloured flowers, and give each a green
 stem printed with the edge of a piece of
 card.

4. When the paint is dry, add a cross stitch
 in the centre of each flower. Glue on a
 border of flowery wallpaper strips.

Note: This makes a lovely card for Mother's Day.

Resist Work

BATIK

The Indonesian art of batik is a process of drawing on fabric with hot melted wax, and then dyeing it - the wax resists the dye.

With young children, it is not always necessary to use a traditional tjanting to apply the wax - paintbrushes are also very effective. It is perfectly acceptable to use melted candle ends with the wicks removed. For melting the wax, a wax pot is best, as the wax is kept safely at the correct temperature. Good results can also be obtained by melting wax in a double saucepan, but care needs to be exercised to keep the wax liquid.

The wax is removed by ironing between several changes of newspaper.

Young children need to be carefully supervised when using hot wax, but, if handled carefully, batik can be appropriate for children as young as four or five.

Free Batik Design

Materials:
White cotton cloth
Melted wax and brushes
Painting dyes, several colours

Method:
1. Paint a design on the cloth with the melted wax.
2. Paint all the spaces in bright colours, using painting dyes.
3. When dry, iron (through newspaper) to remove the wax.

Note: The children may wish to experiment with colours, for example, by over-painting a red section with a yellow dye. The wax lines will keep the colours separate.

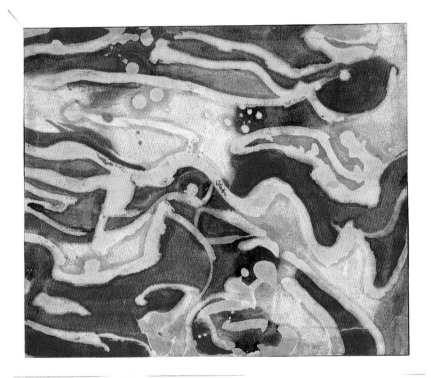

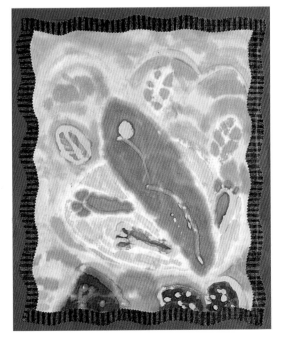

Frog Batik

Materials: As above
Method:
1. Draw the frog outline in wax and add waves, lilypads, bubbles, frogspawn, eyes, etc.
2. Paint with painting dyes.
3. When dry, iron (through newspaper) to remove the wax.

Note: This simple outline idea can be easily adapted to almost any subject - flowers, Autumn leaves, umbrellas, and 'my house' can all be effective.

Batik Babies

Materials:
As for 'Free Batik Design' on facing page

Method:
1. Paint the baby outline in wax on to the cloth. Add details such as features, hair, nappy, etc.
2. Paint on the dyes.
3. When dry, iron (through newspaper) to remove the wax.
4. The borders were made from ruched strips of old net curtains.

Note: These babies were painted as part of a topic on Babies.

Fish Batik

Materials:
White cotton cloth
Melted wax and brushes
Painting dyes -
   concentrated for the fish, diluted for the sea

Method:
1. Paint the fish outline on to the cloth with melted wax. Add wax seaweed, bubbles, waves and fish's eye.
2. Paint the fish with bright dyes and the sea with diluted dyes in blues, greens and purples.
3. When dry, iron (through newspaper) to remove the wax.
4. The work was mounted in a 'weedy' frame: fabric scraps, shells and pebbles were glued to strips of sugar paper. Other details may be added if desired - netting, sequins and beading are very effective.

Embroidered Batik

Materials:
Piece of cotton cloth
Melted wax and brushes
Blue and yellow painting dyes
Sequins, beads and threads
Method:
1. Draw a sun shape in melted wax, add rays and features.
2. Paint on the yellow and blue dyes.
3. When dry, iron (through newspaper) to remove the wax.
4. Decorate with couched threads, stitched on lametta, sequins and beads.
5. Add a frame of strips of white net, tied in knots.

Dipped Batik, Quilted

Materials:
Piece of cotton cloth
Melted wax
Pink dipping dye
Method:
1. Paint the design on the cloth with hot wax - this one was African inspired.
2. Dip the whole cloth in the dye bucket for five minutes.
3. When dry, iron (through newspaper) to remove the wax.
4. If the work is to be quilted, you will need a piece of wadding and a backing cloth the same size as the batik work. Pin and sew the three layers together, with the wadding in the middle. Use the design as a guide to where to stitch.
5. Decorate with whipped running stitches, sequins and beads.

Note: This piece may be made into a cushion if desired, (as shown in photograph).

Cracking

Materials:
Piece of cotton cloth
Melted wax
Painting dye

Method:
1. Wax the cloth all over, using a wide paintbrush.
2. Put it in the fridge for one minute to set it hard.
3. Make controlled cracking patterns by bending and crumpling the cloth. The pattern on the left was made by pressing the cloth around a bottle top, forcing the wax to crack (see line drawing).
The pattern on the right was made by pressing the cloth down over random pencil points. Another pattern could be made by concertina folding, then twisting, the waxed cloth.
4. Use a large paintbrush to work the dye into the cracks on the waxed side. Iron between newspapers to remove wax.
5. The work can be further embellished with stitching or beading if desired.

Note: Ensure the wax used is not adulterated with plastic, or it will not crack properly.

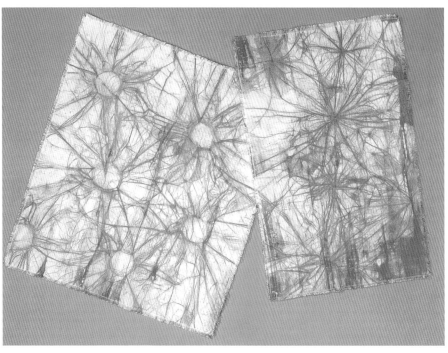

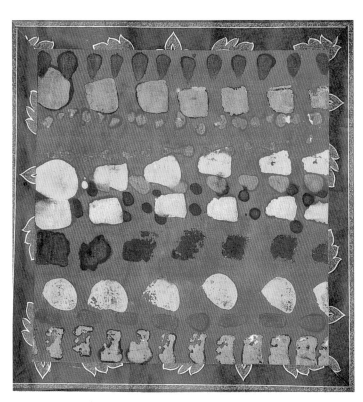

Coloured Waxes

Materials:
Piece of cotton cloth
Egg poacher
Lots of wax crayon stubs
Painting dye
Sponges, brushes, cottonbuds, sticks

Method:
1. Sort the crayons by colour, remove the papers, and put a pile of each colour into the sections of an egg poacher.
2. Boil the water in the poacher and melt the crayons. For safety, wrap an old towel round the poacher when in use.
3. Use old sponge bits and pieces, brushes, cottonbuds, sticks, etc. to dip into the wax, and print rows of repeat patterns on the cloth. The hot water will keep the wax liquid for several minutes.
4. Paint all over with painting dye.
5. Iron between newspapers to remove the wax. Wax crayons have more concentrated pigment than coloured candles, and will colour the cloth well.

Note: This is a good way to use up odd scraps of crayons, but be sure they are wax and not plastic. Melt a good quantity of crayons at a time, as sponges are quite absorbent. If the sponge clogs up with dried wax, either discard it, or dip into hot water to soften it.

Nigerian Starch Resist

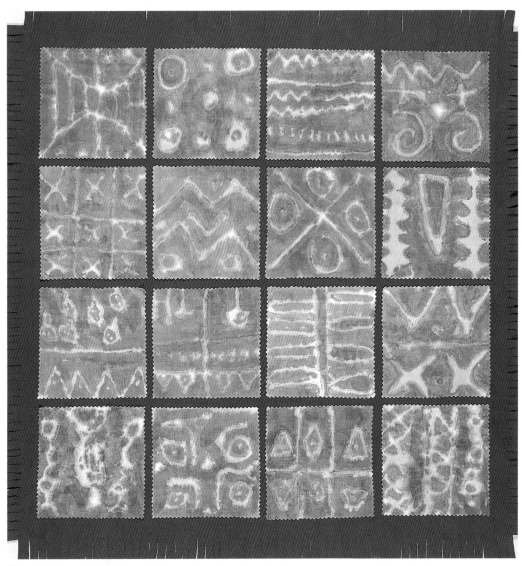

Materials:
Small pieces of cotton cloth
Plain flour and water
A washing-up liquid container
Painting dye in dark blue

Method:
1. Mix plain flour and water to a pancake batter consistency, with no lumps. Put this into the washing-up liquid container.
2. Look at an Adire cloth or a photograph of one. Each child can either choose a pattern to copy or make up his/her own. They might like to practise on paper first.
3. Drizzle the paste on to the cloth in the patterns required.
4. The paste must dry absolutely hard overnight on a flat surface. It will shrink and crack slightly as it dries. If a more cracked effect is required, crumple up the fabric first, then smooth it out.
5. Paint on the dye. It is important not to dip the fabric, as this would make the paste soften, and the dye would creep under it.
6. Iron (through newspaper) to fix the colour.
7. Dampen the cloth and scrape off the paste.
8. Either stitch the squares together and add a border, or pink the edges and glue to a felt background.

Note: Nigerian Yoruba starch resist uses cassava flour, alum and indigo dye, and the whole pattern is worked on a single piece of cloth. Starch resist is a technique that can be used successfully for individual pieces of work such as animals, plants, patterns, etc. The colour effects are subtle and delicate.

Weaving and Winding

Loom Examples

Looms can be made from many things. They may be commercially bought, circular or square notched looms, or may be home-made from a shoebox lid or plastic ice-cream lid. They may be made from notched paper plates or curved pieces of card. You could weave on a forked twig, a bicycle wheel, a wire coat-hanger, a refrigerator shelf, a bent piece of copper pipe, a clothes horse or the upturned legs of a chair. The only criterion is that the warp threads are held taut.

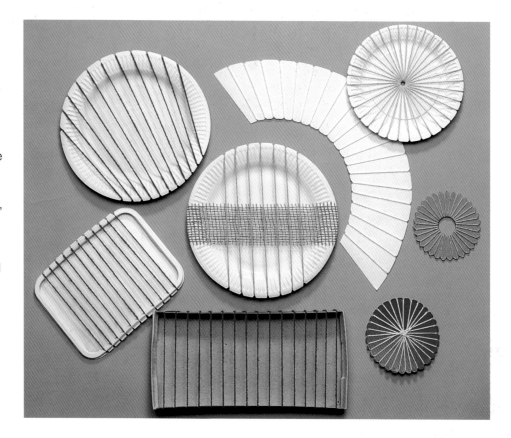

Paper Plate Weaving

Materials:
Notched paper plates
Wool for the warp
Strips of cloth, ribbon, braid, lace, plastic, netting, etc., for the weft

Method:
1. Decide on the shape required - fan, concentric circles, stripes, etc.
2. Cut notches in the plates in appropriate places and wind up the warp threads with wool.
3. Choose fabric strips for the weft, and weave them in and out to achieve the required shape. Tuck or glue odd ends into the back of the work, and trim the edges.
4. Foils, beads, sequins, etc., may be used as decoration.

Note: Do not attempt to remove the weaving from the plate as it will lose its shape. A plate woven in stripes of skin-coloured cloth can be developed into an amusing face by gluing on felt features, ears, fringed or plaited hair, etc.

Dishcloth Weaving

Materials:
Piece of dishcloth
Lengths of ribbon, coloured
    wools, plastic strips, lace,
    braid, beads and small foil
    pieces (for example,
    Shimmer Shower)

Method:
1. Using a curved bodkin,
   thread up lengths of ribbon or
   wool, and weave them in and
   out in lines, following the
   warp of the cloth. The needle
   can be pushed in and out at
   random places along the line.
2. Beads and foil pieces can be
   threaded in and out for further
   texture.

Note: If desired, ribbons can be
decorated with fabric crayon
patterns before weaving. This
work could be made into a bag
by gluing it to a piece of felt the
same size, folding it in half,
sewing up the two sides, and adding a handle.

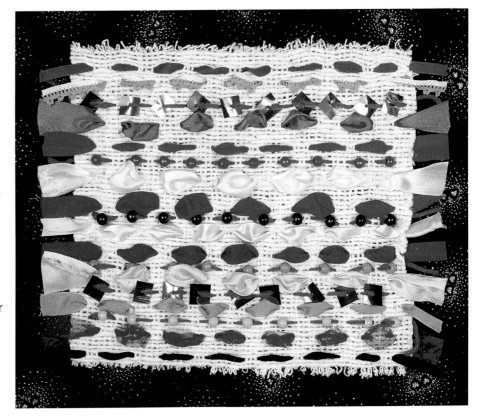

Hessian Weaving

Materials:
Piece of hessian cut
    carefully along the
    warp and weft
Strips for weaving -
    silk, chiffon, ribbon,
    netting, lametta,
    plastic

Method:
1. First, make gaps in
   the hessian by
   pulling out groups
   of threads in the
   warp, two to ten
   threads at a time,
   at random. Make
   similar gaps here
   and there in the
   weft.
2. Weave strips of
   cloth in and out of
   the gaps from side
   to side. Weave
   lametta and plastic in
   and out, top to bottom.
3. Fringe the edges.

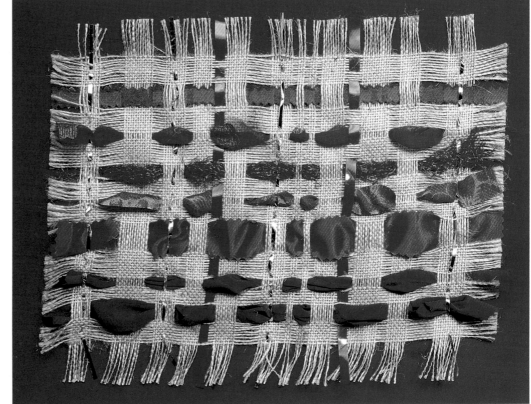

Note: It is important to leave a strong block of threads round the edges when making the gaps in
the hessian.

Spiral Net Weaving

Materials:
Piece of rigid net from a fruit bag
Raffia or thick wool
Felt scraps

Method:
1. Thread up a curved bodkin with raffia or wool, tie a large knot in the end and start at the centre. Weave the raffia in and out of the holes, turning the work as you go to build up a spiral. Glue the end in place.
2. Add felt details – snake head, fish tail, spider, eyes, etc.
3. Staple to a piece of card and add border strips. These borders had running stitches or cross stitches sewn into pre-punched holes.

Note: Fruit and vegetable netting bags can be used in many kinds of artwork, and it is worthwhile building up a good collection of colours. Other ideas to try are:-
– Cut strips of netting and incorporate them into weaving for added texture.
– Green netting strips make excellent seaweed or foliage: the net can be stitched or glued, knotted, twisted or plaited.
– Make a hanging by threading canes through the top and bottom of a large piece of netting, then weaving ribbons, wools, strips of cloth, dried grasses, etc. in and out of the holes.
– Cut a spider web shape from white netting, pin and stitch it to a dark background fabric. Glue on a felt spider and flies and add a few 'dewdrops' of silver glitter glue.

Rainbow Weaving

Materials:

Curved card loom with 20 notches on inside, 20 on outside

Seven strips of cloth in rainbow colours

Silk-sponged background

Method:

1. Wind up the loom with white wool, taping the ends to the back.
2. Thread a bodkin with cloth and weave in and out of the warp threads. Start with violet on the inside of the rainbow shape - natural tension will hold the cloth in place.
3. Glue the ends of the fabric strips to the back.
4. Use in a picture. Here, the sun was woven on a notched plastic lid with glitter thread, and rain was made by sewing on pieces of drinking straws with glitter thread.

Note: Do not cut the warp threads or the weaving will lose its shape.

Weaving with Sheer Fabrics

WARP: made from strips of white and coloured nets and chiffons, taped or stapled to a card frame, top and bottom.

WEFT: made by weaving strips of coloured sheers in and out of the warp. Some of the fabric strips were knotted or twisted, to create a good texture. Tape securely at the sides. Interesting effects occur as various colours overlap.

Cut Paper Looms

Materials:
Piece of A4 card
3cm strips of fabric,
 towelling or other
 stiff, textured cloth
Frame made from
 sugar paper
Felt scraps, feathers,
 pipecleaners

Method:
1. Fold the A4 card in
 half lengthways.
 Make cuts along it
 at 3cm intervals, to
 within 3cm of the
 long edge. Open
 out.

2. Weave the fabric
 strips in and out of
 the slits to give a
 check design. Glue the ends in place.
3. Make the animal frame by drawing the shape on to sugar paper and cutting away the centre. The centre
 cut-out must be no larger than 16cm x 24cm.
4. Glue the weaving behind the animal frame and trim off the corners.
5. Add felt and feathers for features, hooves, etc.

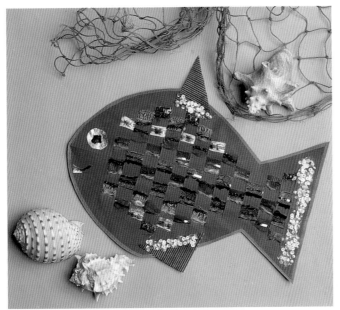

Note: Paper looms may have paper strips woven into them, but fabric gives a more interesting texture. It is possible to cut slots directly in the paper or card outline, as with this fish. Fold the paper lengthways, cut out a symmetrical fish and make snips along the fold. Weave lengths of sparkly fabrics, wools and lametta in and out of the slots, building up a good texture.

Sea Weaving

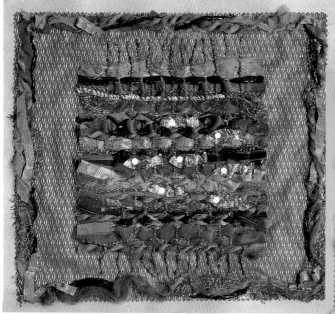
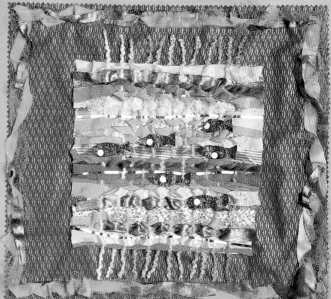

Materials:
Re-usable notched card loom
Fabric strips in blues, greens and purples, netting and lurex strips
Blue wools

Method:
1. Wind up the loom with blue wool.
2. Weave strips of cloth, thick wools, lurex and netting, in and out of the warp, trying to achieve a good mix of textures. Push the rows together as you work, so there are no gaps.
3. Cut the warp threads at the back, remove the loom and immediately glue a piece of card to the back of the weaving. This will stabilise the threads and fabric so they will not move.
4. Neaten the edges of the threads and fabric strips. Glue on foil or felt fish and mount as desired.

Note:
1. You may prefer, at stage 3, to tie the warp threads together in pairs and glue the fabric edges under. The card backing will then not be needed.
2. This idea is adaptable to make backgrounds of any kind - sky, jungle, garden, polar, city, etc.

Free Weaving

Materials: as above
Method: As above, except that the strips do not need to be in complete rows. You may turn at any point, building up curving blocks of colour for the waves. Leave the side threads loose, tying in a few extra if there are any gaps. Cut the warp threads, tie to canes and stabilise the back with card. Glue on seaweed, shells, etc.

Woven Pictures - Day and Night

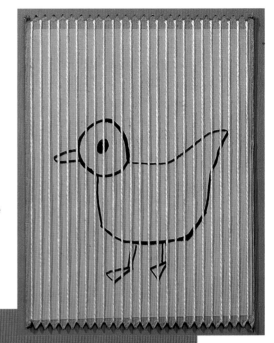

Materials:

Notched card loom 15cm x 20cm
Strips of coloured cloth 25cm long
Coloured wools, curved bodkin
Oddments of felt, dried grasses, feathers, pipe-cleaners

Method:

1. Wind up the warp threads - light for daytime, dark for night-time.
2. Draw a simple outline with black felt-tip pen on a piece of paper 15cm x 19cm, and slide this behind the warp threads. This gives the pattern for the weaving (see photograph at right).
3. First weave inside the picture outline with coloured wools. Build up the rows over your outline, taking care when you turn at the edges not to pull the wool too tightly. Overlap the wools when joining in a new piece, and tuck stray ends behind the weaving.

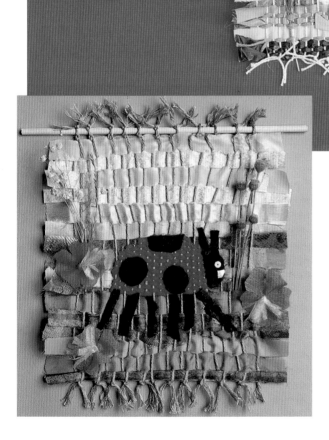

4. When the central outline is completed, weave the background. Choose fabric strips of the appropriate colour, and weave from one side of the loom to the other, leaving the ends loose at the sides. Pass the needle behind the central picture, each time you come to it.
5. Glue on details such as legs, eyes, etc. Reeds, grasses and feathers can be pushed directly into the weaving.
6. Remove the loom by cutting the warp threads at the back and tying them together in pairs, or to a piece of cane.
7. The side edges may be left loose or glued to the back. Gluing card to the back will stabilise the weaving.

Dragonfly Mesh Weaving

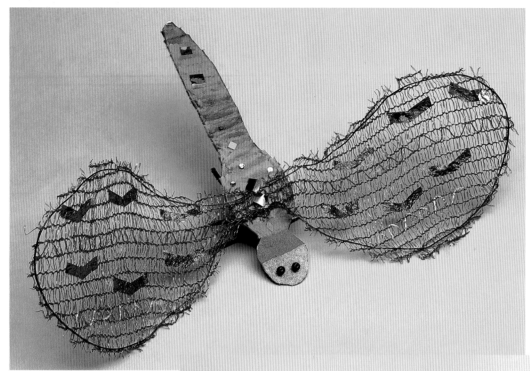

Materials:
Pieces of onion bag mesh
Flexible black wire
Stiff card for body
1¹/₂ cm strips of shiny
   cloth
Decorations - threads,
   sequins, foils,
   Cellophane, pipe-
   cleaners

Method:
1. Draw the body on the card, cut it out, and wrap strips of shiny cloth firmly around it, carefully gluing the ends. Decorate with sequins, eyes and three folded pipecleaners for legs.
2. Fold the mesh in half and cut out symmetrical wings, leaving them attached at the centre.
3. Weave a length of wire in and out of the mesh, close to the outside edge. Make each wing with a separate piece of wire. Twist the wire ends firmly together at the centre, using pliers.
4. Decorate the wings with stitches, foils, etc.
5. Stitch or staple the wings to the thorax. The dragonfly may be free-standing or hung as a mobile.

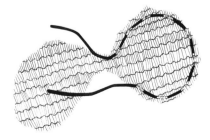

Group Weaving

Materials:
Multi-coloured fabric
    strips
Body loom made from a
    large piece of stiff
    card
Arm looms made from
    shoebox lids
Strong wool

Method:

1. First make the three
   looms. Snip small
   notches along the
   long edges of the
   card and the long
   edges of the shoebox
   lids. Wind strong
   wool around the
   notches.
2. Weave strips of cloth
   in and out of the warp
   threads, pushing the
   strips together to
   achieve a good
   texture. Each child
   can weave a row or
   two, choosing his/her
   own colours.
3. Remove the looms
   carefully by snipping
   two warp threads at a
   time at the back, and
   tying them securely
   in pairs.
4. Glue card to the back
   of the three pieces of
   weaving to stabilise
   it, and tape under the
   edges of the warp
   and weft.
5. Draw round a child's
   hands and feet, paint
   them and cut them
   out. Paint a head with
   the same skin tones.
6. Assemble by gluing
   all the parts on to a
   piece of hessian.

Note: This weaving was inspired by the story of Joseph's coat of many colours. Other suitable stories might be *The Patchwork Quilt* by Valerie Flournoy, Picture Puffin (use a simple rectangular card loom), or the 'Elmer' stories by David McKee (Anderson Press). (For the elephant, use a rectangle for the body and two shoe box lids for the legs. Details of trunk, ears and tail can be cut from felt and glued on.)

God's Eyes

Materials:
Two pieces of thin dowelling
Assorted strips of torn fabrics and wools in chosen colours (you may incorporate lengths of ribbon, lace, nets, etc.)

Method:
1. Tie the sticks together at the centre very firmly with strong thread.
2. Tie the first length of cloth to the centre and begin winding. (Right-handers may prefer to work in an anti-clockwise direction, and left-handers in a clockwise direction.) Wind the cloth under and around each stick in turn, keeping the cloth fairly taut.

3. Tie in the next colour when required, keeping the joins at the back. The pattern will build up into squares. Tie up and neaten the ends at the back, when the pattern is large enough.

Note: A restricted range of colours works well, for example, red, orange and yellow. You may wish to decorate the work further, with tassels, feathers, etc.

Collage Weaving

Materials:
A discarded refrigerator shelf (as loom)
Assorted torn fabric strips and wools

Items to weave in:
feathers, curtain hooks and rings, belt buckles, buttons, Cellophane strips, sticks, poppy seed heads, paper umbrellas, squares of netting, dried flowers, strips of lace or tulle, tassels, bamboo strips, large beads

Method:
Tie a piece of cloth to the side edge. Weave it in and out to the other side and tie it there. Continue

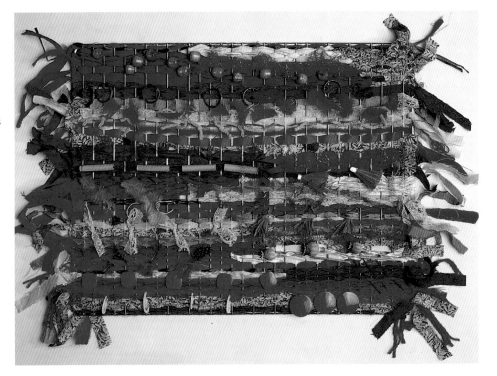

with further strips of cloth and wools, building up a good texture and colour mix. With some strips, you may choose to go part-way only, then turn back to the starting point, resulting in blocks of colour here and there, rather than straight lines. Items may be woven in during the weaving, or afterwards.

Note: A colour theme helps to integrate the weaving. (The theme in the weaving shown is Warm Colours.) You might like to choose all-natural or all man-made items to weave in.

Creative Stitching

Four Seasons

Materials:
Piece of oatmeal hessian
Oddments of white and coffee lace, and flowered
  net curtain
Strips of string and white braid for the trees
Felt pieces

Method:
1. Choose a season and decide what features to include.
2. Cut out felt shapes for flowers, a snowman or a sun. Cut out flower or butterfly shapes from the net curtains or lace. Open up the braiding to make tree branches.
3. Assemble all the pieces you need and arrange them on the hessian. Stitch the pieces down and add further stitching where necessary. For example, the sun's rays could be straight stitches or pieces of drinking straws stitched down. Snow was made from circles cut from lace curtain, and grass was felt or braid.
4. Add wallpaper or foil borders.

Note: This method was successfully used for a series of work on the weather, using weather symbols such as sun, snow, cloud, wind, lightning. These were stitched on to carefully chosen printed fabrics - sparkly for snow, swirly for wind, etc. Small figures could be added, dressed in felt clothing appropriate for the weather.

Iron-on Fabric Flowers

Materials:

Scraps of satin
  materials,
  various colours
Fabric bonding
  (e.g. *Bondina*
  or *Bondaweb*)
Sequins, beads,
  embroidery
  threads
Plain background
  materials
Real flowers for
  observation

Method:

1. First, prepare the satin scraps by ironing them on to a bonding backing. This enables the children to cut crisp edges from fabric that frays. It incorporates an adhesive backing, so it can be ironed into place and stitched as required.
2. Look carefully at the flower and draw its shape on to the paper backing of the Bondina. The rhododendron flowers were cut out whole. The pansy and clematis had the petals individually cut out.
3. Arrange the cut flowers, leaves and petals on the plain background material.
4. Peel off the paper on the back of each petal, leaf or flower, and iron over the whole design. Each piece of satin cut out will now be bonded to the background material.
5. Add details of stems, stamens and leaf veins using stitches and beads.

Note: Bonded material can be used to make a personalised birthday card (for example, 'S' for Sarah) or Mother's Day card ('M' for Mother). Cut a large letter from a piece of bonded material, remove the backing paper and iron it on to a piece of fabric. Decorate the letter with stitching, beads or sequins and glue the work to the front of a folded card.

Felt Fruit

Materials:
Fruit and vegetables for close observation
Felt in assorted colours
Calico or similar for background
Beads, wheat, lentils, curtain hooks, etc., for seeds
Ric-rac braid

Method:
1. Look at the cut fruit or vegetable carefully, noticing the shapes, colours and seeds.
2. Draw the outline shape directly on to the felt, and cut it out.
3. Draw and cut from felt the inside shapes you need, choosing the colours carefully, and placing strips of felt round the edges or inside, where necessary. The overall general impression is more important than very fine detail.
4. Stitch the main piece of felt on to the calico. The smaller pieces and edging strips may be stitched and glued into place.
5. Glue on the 'seeds' as appropriate to create the desired effect. Additional stitching, for example, seeding, may be added as required.

Note:
1. Other suitable fruits to try might be watermelon, lemon, pomegranate, kiwi fruit, or tomato.
2. Cut fruits give beautiful effects when worked in batik or with fabric crayons. Beads and stitching can be added for the internal details.

Frosted Autumn Tree Hanging

Whole class project

Materials:
Long piece of light cloth for
    backing
Same length of wadding
Pieces of light fabrics in blues
    and browns for background
Large piece of felt for the tree
Scraps of felt, wools, braids in
    Autumn colours
Silver glitter

Method:
1. Chalk out the trunk and
   branches on the large piece
   of felt. When you are satisfied
   with the proportions, cut it out
   and turn it over.
2. Stitch, couch or glue pieces
   of wool, braid or chiffon over
   the tree shape. Add sections
   of long stitch here and there.
3. Prepare the background by
   sandwiching the wadding
   between the backing cloth
   and the layers of blues and
   greens. Pin and stitch the
   three layers together to give a
   quilted effect.
4. Sew the tree on to the
   background.
5. Draw and cut out felt leaves
   in Autumn colours and stitch
   them into place along the
   central vein.
6. Cut out felt toadstools and
   stitch them in place. Acorns
   were cut from felt and glued
   on.
7. Add lines of glue along the
   trunk and branches and
   shake on plenty of silver
   glitter, for the frost.
8. Add a border of black felt all
   around the hanging to bond
   all the layers together. The
   name of the school may be
   added in black felt if desired.

Note: This project may be
simplified by using only one
layer of fabric for the
background, with no quilted
effect.

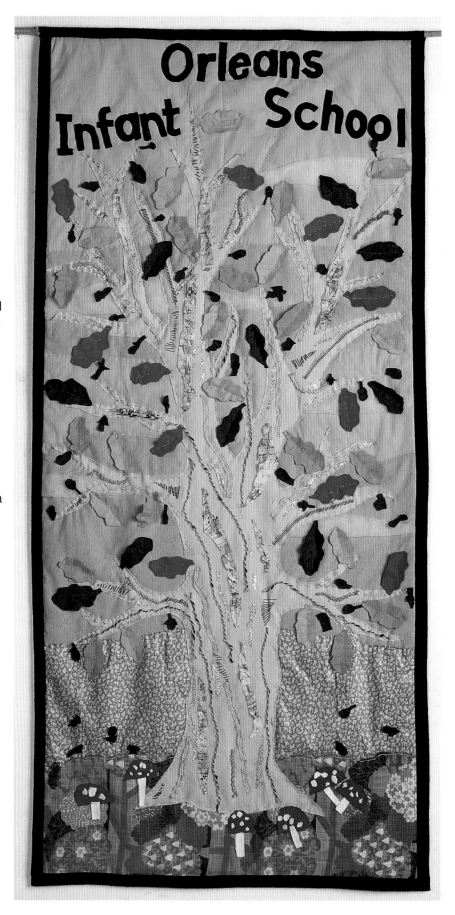

Autumn Feltwork

Materials:
Oddments of felt
Autumn-coloured background cloth (a firm, open weave was used)
Oval card frames
Long pieces of fabric for winding on the frames
Glitter threads
Beads

Method:
1. Look carefully at the basic shapes of dandelion, toadstool, barley and horse-chestnut.
2. Draw the outline shapes on to the felt and cut them out. Turn the felt over so the drawing lines do not show.
3. Stitch the felt on to the background and add details, as approriate:
   – white beads for toadstool spots
   – long stitches for the dandelion head and barley hairs
   – spikes stitched on the horse-chestnut cases
   – couching for stems
   – extra felt details on the horse-chestnuts.
4. Make the frames by winding 2cm strips of fabric around the oval card frame until it is covered. Glue down the ends. Glitter thread may be wound on top, if desired.

Fireworks

Materials:
Felt oddments
Threads, sequins, glitter or glitter glue, stars, beads
Hessian for background
Ric-rac braid, pipe-cleaners

Method:
1. Choose which firework you would like to depict, and cut out the basic shape from felt - cone, rectangle, spiral, rocket, etc.
2. Stitch the main shape on to the hessian.
3. Decorate the picture creatively, with lines of stitches, glued on ric-rac or pipe-cleaners and felt details. Add plenty of sparkle with sequins, glitter or glitter glue.

Note: Fireworks are an inspiration for all kinds of creative work. Coloured wax crayon batik (see page 23) is effective with a dark dye brushed over. Or you might try a tie-dye dark blue sky with bright felts and stitching over.

Octopus Bags

Materials:
Two pieces of felt, twice as long as wide
Beads, pipe-cleaners, tassels, fringes
Felt scraps

Method:
1. Look at examples of Octopus bags and other artefacts made by Native Americans. The bags in the photograph above were based on bags made by Plateau Indians and are named because of the eight tentacles on the fringe. Notice the patterns of beading, flowers, zig-zags, buffalo, fringes, hunting scenes, etc. Sketch out a design on paper.
2. Cut each piece of felt into four sections on the bottom half. These make the tentacles.
3. Decorate one piece of felt with stitched-on details, following the ideas in your design. Incorporate beads, tassels, small felt shapes, stitched-on pipe-cleaners and rows of stitches. The back of the bag may be plain, or decorated to match the front.
4. Stitch the two pieces of felt together along the top half only, allowing the eight tentacles to hang freely. Use overstitches at the sides, and a line of running stitches above the tentacles.
5. Add a handle made from plaited wool or felt strips.

Angel

Materials:
Piece of white satin cloth
Scraps of silver lurex
Blue background material
Decoration - pearl beads, sequins, silver thread, silver wool for hair
Frame (if required) – card cut to shape, pasta and spray paint

Method:
1. Cut out an oblong of white cloth and gather it with running stiches along one edge. Stitch it to the background at the neck.

2. Cut out a circle of white satin for the head, and stitch it down over a piece of wadding.
3. Glue on facial features, arms, hair and wings.
4. Decorate the dress with a long strip of lurex and pearl beads. Cross stitches are sewn on randomly as stars, on the dress and in the sky.
5. The frame is made by gluing pasta shapes to card and spraying silver or gold.

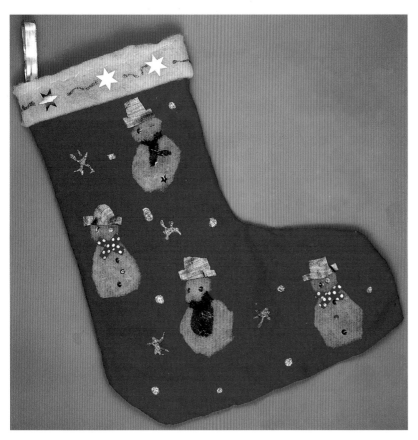

Christmas Stocking

Materials:
Piece of red felt or shiny red cloth
White wadding
Decoration - lurex scraps, sequins, glitter pens

Method:
1. Cut out two stocking shapes from the red cloth (or cut out the stocking in one piece, folded along the straight edge).
2. Decorate with snowmen (cut from wadding) and add hats, scarves and sequins.
3. Stitch up the stocking firmly, right sides together.
4. Turn the right way and stitch a strip of wadding around the top. Decorate with glitter pens and sequin stars.

Note: Other suitable repetitive motifs might be stars, bells or Christmas trees.

Personal Banner

Materials:
Large piece of felt or other
  plain background fabric
Oddments of coloured felt
Fringes, beads, sequins, glitter
  glue, etc., for decoration
Cane for hanging

Method:
1. Design your banner on
   paper first. It should tell
   others about yourself - your
   hobbies, initial, sign of the
   zodiac, birthday, favourite
   food or colour, right or left
   handedness, etc.
2. Draw and cut out from felt all
   the outlines you wish to
   include, and stitch them into
   place. Add a fringe, beads,
   badges, or any other
   decoration you wish.
3. Cut notches in the top of the
   cloth, fold over a cane and
   glue down firmly.

Quilted Umbrella

Materials:
Two pieces of fine polyester/cotton
Small piece of wadding
Fabric crayons

Method:
1. Draw an umbrella outline in pencil on
   thin paper. When you are satisfied with
   the design, colour it carefully with
   fabric crayons, using a different pattern
   for each section of the umbrella.
2. Iron the design on to the fabric.
3. Sandwich an umbrella-shaped piece of
   wadding between the two pieces of
   cloth (design on top) and pin together
   very carefully.
4. Sew running stitches around the
   outline and between the sections,
   making sure you stitch right through all
   the layers. Add a few 'rain' stitches if
   you wish, or beads, or glitter rain.
5. Staple to a piece of card and add a
   border.

Note: Any simple outline can be similarly
quilted: for example, a Christmas bell or
star, an Easter egg or an autumn leaf.

Bookmarks

Cross-stitch Sampler
Stitch a piece of transparent ribbon on to a strip of binca using cross-stitches. The holes will clearly show through the ribbon. Add your initial and fringe the edges.

Poppies
Sponge green and yellow fabric paint on to a strip of neutral material. Print a few green stems with a piece of card edge. Paint on red poppies and add black stitching at the centres. Lightly fringe the edges.

Lace and Ribbon
Cut a strip of net curtain with a hole pattern in it. Weave ribbon through the holes. Stitch on to a rectangle of felt, using whipped running stitch.

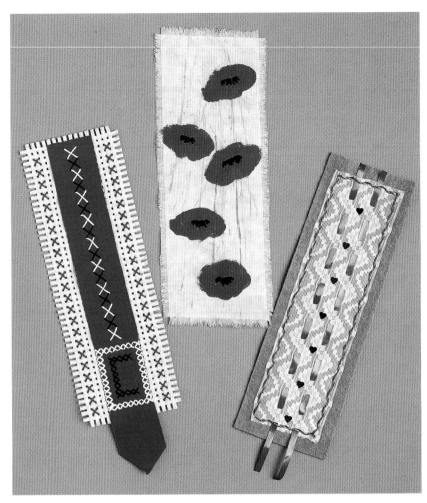

Giraffe
Cut a white felt giraffe head, and appliqué on black spots.

Mermaid
Cut oddments of felt for the head, body and arms, and glue or sew these to a rectangle of felt. Cut a tail from green net and stitch it down. Decorate the tail with stitching, glitter foil, glitter glue and sequins. Sew on green glitter thread hair and glue on sequins for the face and necklace. You may wish to sponge green fabric paint lightly around the mermaid.

Totem Pole
Cut three coloured squares of felt and stitch these on to a rectangle of black felt. Make each square into a face by gluing on coloured foils, feathers and pieces of felt.

Note: Tall or long subjects make very suitable bookmarks - for example, a tree, caterpillar, lighthouse, windmill, rabbit, Christmas candle, clown, Russian doll, clock, church tower, parrot, etc.

Cards and Book Covers

Mother's Day Dyed Flowers

Materials:
Long strip of white
  cotton fabric
  50cm x 9cm
Painting dyes in three
  colours
Felt or fabric scraps for
  leaves and stems

Method:

1. Paint broad stripes of dye colour on the cloth, allowing the colours to blend together. The stripes may be painted vertically or horizontally.
2. When the cloth is dry, pink the long edges and draw a pencil line 2cm from one long edge - this is the sewing line.
3. Sew running stitches along the line, gather up tightly and fasten off.
4. Glue the flower to a piece of folded A4 card, and add leaves and a stem. (The flowers in the photograph were scented with a few drops of rosewater.)

The daffodil and tulips were made in a similar manner. Long strips of cloth are dyed, then cut and gathered up.

The daffodil uses two strips of cloth: one is wider, dyed yellow and cut into six petal shapes; the other is narrow, dyed yellow and orange, and gathered into the trumpet.

The tulips are each made from a single, long piece of cloth, dyed in stripes, then gathered up

Note: The tulips and daffodil trumpets use a shorter length of cloth than the multicoloured flowers or the daffodil petals.

Mother's Day Binca Design

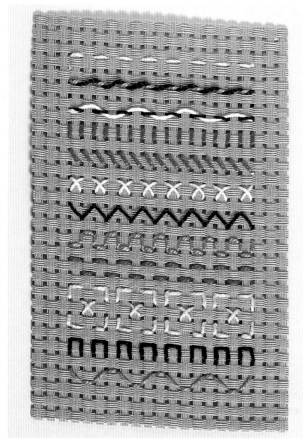

Materials:
Window cards, commercially bought or home-made
Small piece of binca
lcm squared paper

Method:
1. Draw your design on the paper in pencil, choosing from a selection of standard stitches (see left). Start from the centre and work outwards.
2. Add colour to your paper design with felt-tip pens.
3. Transfer the design on to the binca, matching the colours of the threads. Start from the centre and work outwards.
4. Glue the completed work centrally behind the card window.

Note:
1. This idea is easily adaptable for an Easter card. Cut out an egg-shaped window from the card. Decorate the binca with rows of stitches and a ribbon bow, and glue behind the window.
2. For a Christmas card, you could try window cut-outs in the shape of a tree, star, bell or candle, and design a pattern using sparkly threads and sequins. Alternatively, you could draw the Christmas outline directly on to the binca, outline and fill in with stitches, and glue the completed work behind an oval window.

Farm Visit Patchwork Book

Materials:
Large, hessian-covered book
Nine squares of background felt
Two long strips of background felt
Oddments of felt for animals and letters
Beads, wools

Method:
1. Cut the background pieces of felt to size so they fit the front of the book, as in the photograph.
2. Draw and cut out the animal shapes from pieces of felt. Stitch the outlines on to the background squares, and glue on small details - eyes, tails, etc.
3. Draw round letter templates, cut them out and stitch them on to the two long strips of background felt.
4. Sew all the pieces together by hand or machine.
5. Trim the outside edges straight and glue the work to the book cover.

Note: The book shown in the photograph contains photographs, drawings, maps and stories about a class visit to a farm. Sheep's wool, feathers, cattle feed, hay, clover and farm literature are also glued and taped inside.

My House Books

Materials:
Pieces of white cloth
Polystyrene tile
Fabric paint
Felt scraps and assorted oddments for collage

Method:
Each book is an example of various ways to treat the same theme.

> RED AND BLACK HOUSE: Pieces of polystyrene tile are cut into squares, triangles and oblongs for the various parts of the house - roof, door, windows and house. Each part is inked separately with different colours and printed on to the cloth.
>
> RED HOUSE: This is a mono-print. Etch a design into a polystyrene tile with a ballpoint pen, ink the tile with red fabric paint, and print on to the cloth.
>
> FELT HOUSE: Cut the shapes out of coloured felts and applique into place with running stitches and cross stitches.
>
> COLLAGE HOUSE: Cut pieces of plastic mesh and stitch on to the white background. Add matchsticks, plastic off-cuts, lace and dried flowers, stitched and glued into place.

All of these examples may be further decorated with stitching.

Zippy Books

Materials:
Background material
Old zips
Scraps of felt fabric and thick wools
Sequins and beads
Sequin waste

Method:
FOR THE CROCODILE
1. Sew a zip on to a piece of background material. Leave the last 5cm unstitched at the opening end, so the jaws can open and close.
2. Glue on felt legs and stitch on an eye.
3. Sew on small oddments of fabric for the swamp, and add a few sequins.
4. Glue on to the bookcover and write a story about a crocodile.

FOR THE BUTTERFLY
1. Sew the zip on to the background material, leaving the ends open as antennae.
2. Cut out symmetrical wings from sequin waste.
3. Sew the wings on at each side of the zip body.
4. Weave thick wools in and out of the holes around the edges of the wings, and decorate with shiny bits.
5. Glue on to the book cover and write a story about the butterfly life-cycle inside.

Diwali Cards

Materials:
A4 card
Small piece of white silk 15cm x 20cm
Silver outlining agent (e.g. gutta)
Silk paints, sponges and fine brushes
Wooden or plastic board, as a working surface

Method:
1. Look at some Indian fabrics or books with traditional motifs such as peacocks, elephants, mango, birds, fish, flowers, etc.
2. On an A5 piece of paper, draw your design in pencil and go over it carefully with a black felt-tip pen.
3. Put the drawing under the silk. It will show through. Tape the silk to the board so it will not move, The board can then be turned around for easy access to all parts of the design.
4. Practise applying the gutta to paper first, then go over all the lines in the design with the gutta, being careful not to smudge it.
5. Remove the silk and allow the gutta to dry completely, at least overnight.
6. Stretch the silk over a frame and staple it down at the edges. The frame may be an old wooden frame, a card frame or a small shoebox. (Hold down the silk with an elastic band.) It is important that the silk does not touch the work surface when it is being painted.
7. Gently and carefully, paint on the silk paints with small brushes for the details and sponges for the background. The paint will spread naturally into the tiny corners, but will be stopped by the gutta. Allow the children to experiment with colour mixing.
8. When dry, remove and mount the fabric on the A4 card (folded in half).

Tie-Dye Book Covers

Materials:
White cotton cloth 4cm
    wider and longer than A4
Three dipping dyes

Method:
Tie up and dye the cloth as in 'Embroidered Tie-dye', page 9. Glue on to the book cover with a 2cm overlap all round. The covers of these books were chosen to match the story theme of 'Bigger and Bigger'. Similarly, a marbled cover could be used for a book about water, the sea or space. A piece of batik or starch resist would make a lovely cover for a story about an animal or insect.

Christmas Tree Cards

PASTA ON HESSIAN
Cut a triangle of hessian. Glue on rows of pasta shapes. Spray with silver or gold paint. Glue on to the card.

GATHERED SATIN
Gather a piece of green satin on one edge. Attach this to the card with a stitch. Then sew on three rows of red beading by putting a stitch at each end of the rows, right through the card. Tape down the ends of the thread inside. Decorate further if desired.

FELT AND RIBBON
Cut out a green felt tree. Stitch around the edge with large stitches. Thread gold ribbon in and out of the stitches and glue down the ends. The star is a piece of gathered ribbon. Glue on to the backing card. Decorate with glitter glue, sequins and glitter.

GOLD LACE
Spray a triangle of lace or open-weave fabric with gold paint. When dry, sew the lace on to the card with random large 'stitches' of gold braid or curling ribbon. Use a very large needle to ensure the holes in the card are big enough for the braid. Use adhesive tape to hold the ends inside the card, and decorate with sequins and gold glitter.

Snowmen Cards

SEWING CARD

Draw a snowman on card. Make needle holes all around the edge. Sew whipped running stitch through the holes using glitter thread. Cut out the snowman and glue it on to a background of net sky and lurex snow. Glitter glue will hold down the net.

PADDED CIRCLES

Cut out two circles of white satin. Stitch on beads and sequins. Stitch on to the background (as on page 56) and add a scarf and hat. This background is cracked batik (see page 23), cracked around a pencil point.

WEAVING

Draw a snowman outline and put this under a loom wound with glitter thread. Weave torn strips of white satin from side to side over the outline.
Glue on a felt hat, scarf, buttons, etc. Cut the threads at the back, remove from the loom and tape down all the loose ends at the back of the weaving. 'Snow' is tiny polystyrene balls.

SCREEN-PRINTING

Block off the screen to A5 size. Fold a piece of A5 paper in half lengthways and cut out a symmetrical snowman. Discard the cut-out. Use the frame as a stencil to print (as on page 14), using white paint on blue cloth. Decorate with glitter and polystyrene balls.

Valentine Cards

PADDED HEART

Cut a heart-shaped window from a folded card. Glue lace around the cut edge, pinching it together here and there to add fullness. Draw the same size heart on to red fabric and cut out two pieces of fabric 2cm larger than the heart. Lightly pad and pin the two hearts together, with a strip of lace across the front. Stitch, using the drawn line as a sewing line. Glue the heart behind the window and decorate.

FELT HEART

Cut a heart shape from red felt. Stitch ready-gathered ribbon around the edge. Advanced sewers might try gathering red net and stitching this round the edge (as in the right-hand version). Glue on to a card and decorate as desired.

WOVEN WINDOW HEART

Cut a heart-shaped window from a folded card. Cut a piece of silver sequin waste as wide as the card and weave strips of red fabrics, ribbons, chiffon, lurex and wools in and out of the holes, in rows. Trim the edges and tape behind the window. Add a border of red ribbon or crêpe paper, glued and pinched round the window, and decorate.

Note: This idea adapts well to an Easter card using an egg-shaped window cut-out.

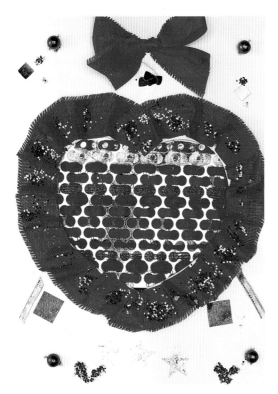

NET AND BEADS HEART

Cut a heart shape from a piece of pretty curtain net. Pin this to a piece of red satin (or other shiny cloth) and stitch it down. Each running stitch has been interspersed with a red bead. Use pinking shears to cut the red satin into a heart shape. Glue on to card and decorate.

Texture and 3-Dimensional Work

Unravelled String

Materials:
Background fabrics (blue, green)
Piece of rope or thick string
Flowered net curtain
Scraps of felt

Method:
1. Glue the background fabrics on to strong paper, for the sky and grass.
2. Unravel the rope to make an interesting tree shape, and use plenty of PVA glue to stick it down on to the fabric.
3. Glue on other details - net curtain flowers, felt sun and people, etc.

Note: Unravelled string makes wonderful hair.

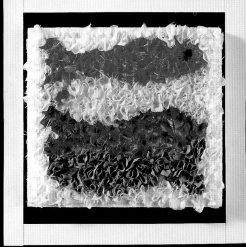

Tufting

Materials:
Square of 1cm thick polystyrene
Odd bits of silky fabrics
(In making these designs shown, the children first looked at designs on an Inca rug, then chose an outline to draw on the polystyrene. Bird, snake, fish, duck, frog, etc., are all traditional designs).

Method:
1. Draw your design on a polystyrene square.
2. Cut up the fabrics into 2cm² pieces, keeping the same colours together.
3. Push the pieces of cloth into the polystyrene using the end of a ballpoint pen. Gradually build up the picture, pushing in the fabric pieces close together with no spaces.

Note: This method works well for flowers in concentric circles.

Padded Shapes

Materials:
Circle or oval of felt
Small piece of wadding or cotton wool
Background fabric
Decorative details - felt oddments, seeds, feathers, braid, shells, seaweed, glitter, pipecleaners, twigs, etc.

Method:
1. Pin the felt circle to the background fabric with the wadding underneath. It is important that the background fabric is flat and the felt is curved over the wadding.
2. Stitch around the edge with running stitches.
3. Glue or sew on any decorative details you wish.

Note:
This padded shape idea can be used as part of a topic on Shape. Geometric shapes of all kinds can be cut from felt and might be made into people, by adding features, arms and legs. The kind of house used by each shape person could also be padded.

For example, Tracy Triangle lives in a triangular house (teepee).
Oliver Oblong lives in an oblong house (block of flats).
Stephen Square lives in a square house.
Cynthia Circle lives in a circular house (igloo), etc.

Rainbow Fringe Caterpillar

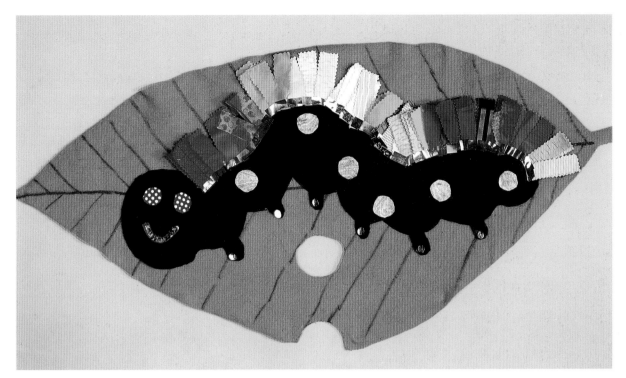

Materials:
Black and green felt
Fabric oddments (thin fabrics) in rainbow colours, several shades of each colour
Small pieces of coloured foil (e.g. *Shimmer Shower*)

Method:
1. Use a white pencil to draw, on the black felt, eight overlapping circles, gradually decreasing in size. Draw the legs and cut out the caterpillar.
2. Turn over the felt. Sort out the fabrics and choose a selection of reds - the children might like to order them, darkest to lightest. Omitting the first circle, stitch strips of folded red fabrics to the top of the next circle, then orange, yellow, etc., one colour for each circle.
3. Glue a row of coloured foil pieces along the stitch line, and glue on details of face and spots.
4. Cut a large leaf from felt, and glue or stitch on the caterpillar.

Note: It is best to use thin fabrics and a fine needle, since there are several thicknesses of cloth to stitch through. This idea could be a cover for a class book on life-cycles.

Woolly Animals

Rabbit: Draw an outline on card and glue wool round and round from outside to centre.
Polar Bear: Cut up an old white woolly jumper into 2cm wide lengths and glue on to an outline as with the rabbit.
Sheep: Knit a small rectangle of woolly knitting (older children only), and stitch on felt details.
Teddy: Draw a teddy outline and put it under the warp threads of a small rectangular loom. Weave wool from side to side over the outline (see Woven Snowman, page 53).

Christmas Tree Decorations

1. **Angel:** Make from a long rectangle of lacy net curtain. Gather with running stitches along a line two-fifths of the way along the fabric, and fasten off. Glue a card head to the top part, add pipe-cleaner arms, tinsel halo.

2. **Beads and Balls:** Ball is made from a circle of red satin, gathered with running stitches round the edge, and stuffed with a cottonwool ball. Beads are made from strips of lurex or satin glued and rolled over a stick. Thread all together with pearl beads . (**Note**: Rolled fabric beads make wonderful necklaces.)

3. **Heart:** Cut two heart outline frames from white card. Sandwich a piece of sparkly net between the frames, glue and trim off the excess. Decorate the frame. (**Note**: This works well with any Christmas outline.)

4. **Candle:** Cut a strip of ribbon, glue on fabric holly leaves and lurex flame. Decorate with glitter and beads.

5. **Tree:** Pin together two roughly cut pieces of green satin over a triangle of foam. Mark a triangle in pencil for the stitching line, using running stitches whipped with glitter thread. Pink the edges and decorate.

6. **Star:** Cut two triangles from sequin waste and overlap them to make a star. Thread red ribbon in and out of the holes.

7. **Santa Face:** Cut two tear-drop shapes from red felt, stitch together and stuff lightly. Glue on a beard and features cut from felt.

8. **Woven Star:** Wind up a small circular loom with lametta. Weave yellow wool in and out around the centre. Cut off the threads at the edges and glue shiny card to the back.

9. **Bell:** Cut two bell shapes from silver lurex. Stitch together, right sides facing, leaving a small gap. Turn the right way, stuff lightly, and sew up the gap. Glue on sequins, beads and a glittery clapper made from a poppy seed head.

10. **Stocking:** Cut two pieces of felt to shape. Stitch around the edges, leaving the top open. Stitch on an edging of fur and decorate with sequins. Add a felt teddy and a pipe-cleaner candy stick.

Felt Sampler

Materials:
Triangle of green felt
Strips of white felt 1cm, 1¹/₂cm, 2cm
    wide
Red satin background
Glitter

Method:
1. Experiment first with the strips of felt - try knotting, plaiting, twisting, looping, twisting two together, curling, tying bows, gathering, etc.
2. Stitch or glue the felt strips in rows on to the felt triangle, using any techniques you like.
3. Add a border of felt snipped into a fringe, and glue on loops and glitter.

Russian Feltwork

A project for ten children

Materials:
One square of felt per child
10 geometric templates (circle, star, pentagon, etc.)
Backing felt

Method:
1. Draw round a shape template on paper, cut it out and fold exactly along the central axis.
2. Fold the felt square in half and put the folded paper shape along the fold of the felt. Draw and cut out the shape from the felt.
3. Cut a smaller shape inside the first cut-out, keeping the felt folded.

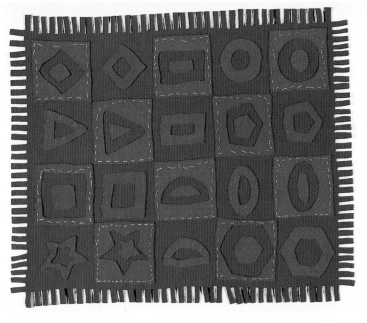

4. Arrange all the felt pieces on the background, so that the cut-out pieces are adjacent to the original square.
5. Pin and stitch down the felt pieces and fringe the border.

Bonding

Materials:
Piece of neutral fabric
Piece of fabric bonding
Piece of white net
Scraps for decoration

Method:
1. Iron the fabric bonding to the neutral fabric and remove the paper.
2. Arrange tiny scraps on the bonded side of the fabric. You may use sequins, glittery wools or threads, small bits of coloured nets, tiny beads, tiny cuttings of tinsel, small bits of coloured foils, etc.
3. When you are satisfied with your arrangement, carefully place a piece of white net over it, cover with paper, and iron. All

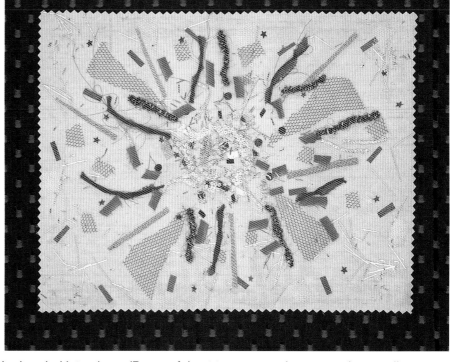

the small decorative bits will be bonded into place. (Be careful not to sneeze when arranging small pieces!)

Note: It is important not to build up too thick a layer of decoration, or it may not bond properly. The work may be further stitched, if desired. This method could make excellent fireworks, with sparkly pieces bonded to a dark background fabric.

The bonding technique can be easily used by very young children, who enjoy arranging patterns within a shape, for example, an egg shape (for an Easter card), or a star shape (for a Christmas card). Fragile leaf skeletons and delicate pressed flowers can also be bonded on to fabric to make beautiful cards and calendars.

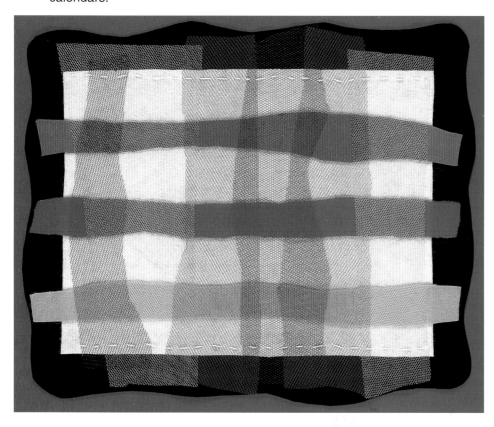

Felt and Net Overlay

Materials:
Rectangle of white felt
Felt oddments in primary colours
Nets in primary colours

Method:
1. Cut three strips of felt in yellow, blue and red, and glue these to the white felt.
2. Cut two strips each of yellow, blue and red net - wavy cutting is more interesting than straight.
3. Arrange the net pieces over the felt, allowing them to overlap. Fascinating colour effects develop.
4. Pin the net in place and stitch it down at the edges. Glue to a black background.

Rippling

Making Waves: Use a selection of thin fabrics in your chosen colours (these were all spotty). Apply PVA glue liberally to card, a section at a time. Put a piece of fabric on and push it into waves in any direction.

Raindrop Mobile

Materials:
Small pieces of ready-marbled fabric
Soft wadding
Glitter thread
Silver foil, white card

Method:
1. Make a raindrop template and draw round this on to the marbled fabric. Cut two raindrops 1cm larger than the drawn outline.
2. Pin the two pieces of fabric together, with a little wadding in between. Stitch along the drawn line in running stitch, and whip this with glitter thread.
3. Pink the edges and attach a silver thread for hanging.
4. Make a cloud from white card with silver foil on both sides, and tape on the raindrops.

Felt Windows

Materials:
Two squares of felt
Oddment of fabric for the roof

Method:
1. Practise cutting out window and door shapes on paper first. Fold the paper and make snips from the fold. Open the snips and press down the flaps.
2. When you have decided on the shape and position of the doors and windows, cut them from felt, folding and snipping in appropriate places.
3. Put the cut piece of felt over the uncut piece and stitch down the flaps.
4. Glue on a roof and paper people at the windows.

Felt and Pasta

Materials:
Piece of card
Oddments of yellow felt
Pasta or pulses
Gold spray

Method:
1. Cut out a circle of felt and glue it to the centre of the card.
2. Cut out and glue on eyes, nose and mouth, or glue on pasta. Don't forget to add 3-dimensional eyelashes.
3. Cut out and glue triangles and strips of felt for the sun's rays.
4. Glue on a pasta border and spray thoroughly with gold paint. Add a little glitter before the spray dries.

Backgrounds

Garden Background

Materials:
Circular piece of dyeing (as on
    page 9)
Hessian threads
Flowery material

Method:
1. Cut up the dyed circle of fabric
   into sections – half a circle for the
   body, and triangles for the tail,
   beak and feet.
2. Assemble the sections on a piece
   of paper and glue down.
   Alternatively, the sections could
   be stitched directly to the
   background cloth.
3. Extra decoration – feathers,
   beads, stitching – could be
   added.
4. Cut a nest shape from paper,
   cover with hessian threads and
   glue into place, with some fabric
   eggs.

Note: A carefully chosen
background fabric is effective just as
it is, or it can be decorated with
collage, stitching, glitter pens,
printing, fabric crayons, etc.

Printed Landscape

Materials:
Three layers of fabric - blue, brown,
    green
White towelling (lamb) and brown
    hessian (tree)
Items for printing - corrugated card
    (fields), potato (flower, leaf) and toilet
    tube (sky)

Method:
1. Glue or stitch the fabric layers to a
   backing paper.
2. Make printing pads with powder paint -
   white, brown, yellow and green - and
   print the layers of the landscape.
3. Cut out a towelling lamb and glue
   down.
4. Cut a length of hessian into strips
   halfway along its length and glue into
   place for the tree. Add tissue blossom.

Beanbag Target

Materials:

Target cloth – 1 metre square
Beans or pebbles for beanbags
Green, yellow and white felt
Oddments of blue, green and brown fabric
Brightly coloured buttons

Method:

FOR THE BEANBAGS

1. Cut out two ovals of felt for the frog (green) or the egg (white), and two circles of felt for the sun (yellow).
2. Cut out legs for the frog, rays for the sun and a chick for the egg.
3. Sew on the button eyes (frog only), then stitch the two felt shapes firmly together, leaving a small gap to be filled with beans. Sew up the gap, and stitch or glue on all the other details.

FOR THE TARGET

1. Glue or stitch on to the target cloth blue fabric for the sky and flowered fabric for the grass. Stitch on a few ragged net clouds.
2. Tear strips of blue and green fabric and glue into a ripple effect for the pond.
3. Stitch on felt reeds, a felt duck and unravelled hessian for the nest.

Enjoy some target practice - try to throw the sun in the sky, the frog in the pond, and the egg in the nest. The target can be rolled up when not in use.

Underwater Tie-Dye and Batik

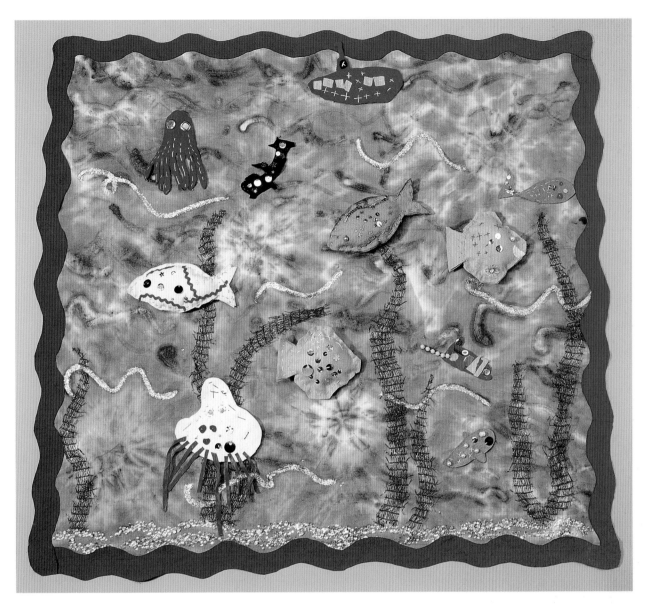

Materials:
Large piece of cotton sheeting
Melted wax and brushes
Blue and green painting dyes
Glitter, sequins, green vegetable mesh
Felt fish and sea creatures decorated with stitching and beading

Method:
1. Paint melted wax in wavy lines all over the cloth.
2. Tightly tie up the cloth in four or five circles (as in 'Tie-dye chick' on page 9), to create circular resist areas here and there.
3. Paint all over with dyes using decorators' paintbrushes.
4. When dry, remove the ties and iron the cloth between newspapers to remove the wax.
5. Decorate with stitched-on mesh seaweed and wavy lines of glitter. Add the fish.

Note:
1. A large piece of tie-dye in dark blue makes an excellent night sky for fireworks.
2. If tied in yellows, browns and reds, it makes an Autumn background for hibernating animals and leaves.
3. Shades of blue make a sky background for birds or hot air balloons.
4. Greens make a jungle or garden.
5. An interesting effect may be obtained by joining individual children's work in a patchwork.

Hessian Background

Materials:
Coarse hessian, frayed at the edges
Strips of bark peeling
Plasticine - pink, white and green -
   for the flowers

Method:
1. Look at some flowering blossom, for example, cherry, apple or quince, noticing the petals and shape of the twig.
2. Tear up the bark peeling and glue it to the hessian in a pleasing twig shape.
3. Make the blossom by rolling the Plasticine into five 1cm balls, and flattening each to make a petal. Press the five balls lightly together and add a stamen.
4. Press the blossoms into the hessian - they should stay put without any glue.

Space

Materials:
Piece of black velvet
Scrap of marbled or swirly patterned fabric
Glittery decoration - tinsel, stars, lurex, sequins, glitter, glue, pipecleaners, etc.

Method:
1. Cut a circle from the marbled fabric. Pin and stitch it to the velvet.
2. Have fun decorating Space extravagantly with stars, moons, planets, comets and rockets. The velvet background is a wonderful foil to the sparkle.
3. Make a card frame and glue crushed kitchen foil around it.

Note: One picture was made of each of the planets for a project on space.

Snow Stencils

Batik Snowflake Stencils:
Cut circles from sticky-backed plastic, fold them into six sections, and cut out snips to make 'snowflake' templates. Peel off the backing and stick the snow stencils to a large piece of white cloth. Apply melted wax to the snowflakes. Remove the stencils and dye the whole cloth with blue painting dyes. Add a snowman made with cottonwool balls and glitter.

Lace Stencil:
Put a piece of lace over some blue cloth and spray all over with silver spray paint. Remove and discard the lace. Add a felt collage skier.

Background Using Sheers

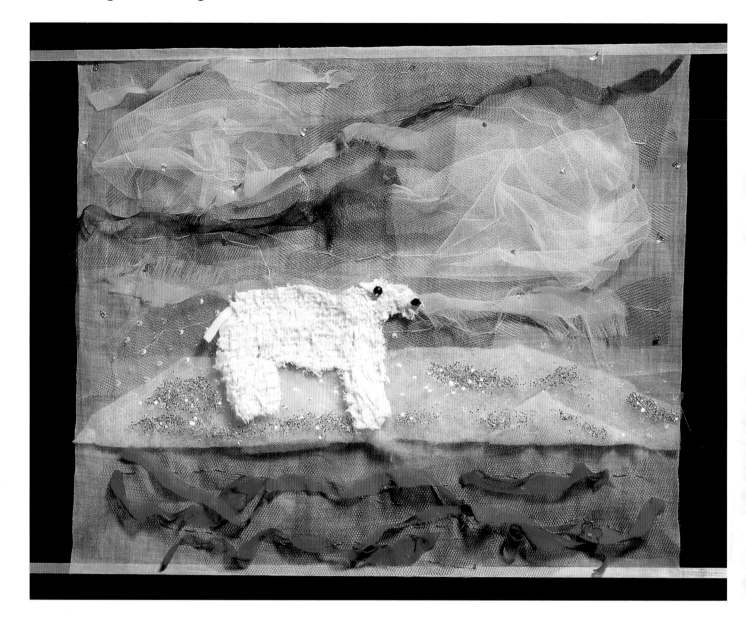

Materials:
Piece of fine muslin for background
Oddments of nets and fine chiffons - blues, greens, whites
Beads, glitter decoration
Polar bear woven on a loom with strips of white cloth (see Snowman, page 53)

Method:
1. Cut up the nets and chiffons into wavy shapes and pin all the pieces on to the muslin. Overlap randomly.
2. Use a fine needle and thread to stitch down the pieces, allowing the needle to meander here and there. You may wish to use glitter thread or sew sequins in as you stitch. Other strips may be lightly glued on randomly.
3. Add some clouds by screwing up pieces of white net and stitching them down here and there.
4. Add any further details you wish - polar bear, glitter, lace snowflakes, etc.

Note: This works well with sea and sky backgrounds.

Woven Backgrounds

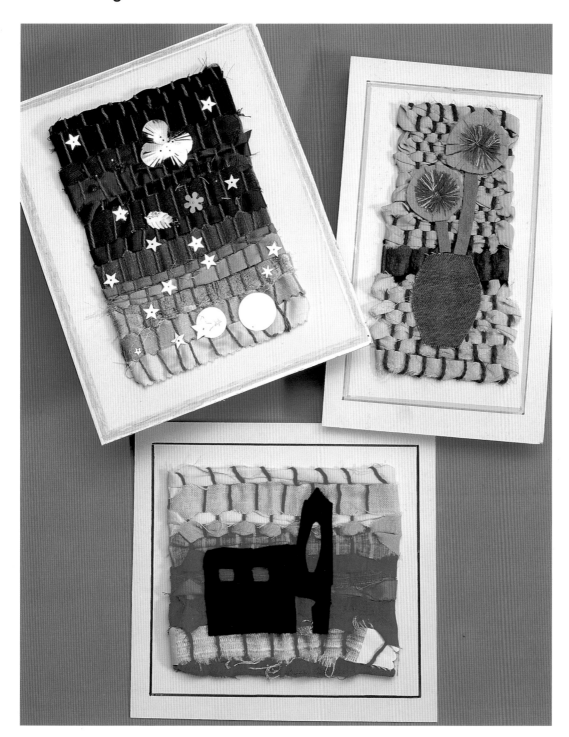

Materials:
Card loom wound with wool
Strips of cloth, curved bodkin
Decoration: sequins, black felt, oddments of various materials

Method:
1. Wind the looms with blue for 'Starry Night', red for the 'Sunset Sky', and brown for 'Sunflowers'. The colours were based on a study of paintings by van Gogh and Monet.
2. Weave the cloth in strips from side to side. The edges can be glued under, tied off or left loose.
3. Use the weaving as a background to glue on details – star sequins, black felt silhouettes, felt flowers.

Note: The sunset sky is very appropriate as a background for 'Fire' - for example, a black felt fireman, building or fire engine against the reds.

Jungle Collage

Materials:
Piece of background material
Fabric paints - blue, several shades of green
Sponges
Oddments of felt, and green patterned or flowered materials
Scraps of green vegetable net, raffia, ribbon, chiffon, tassels

Method:
1. Sponge the fabric paint on to the cloth - blue at the top and shades of green at the bottom. Sponge tree shapes and plant shapes in various greens. Fill in any spaces with watery paint.

2. Cut out felt animals – tiger, zebra, lion, monkey, birds, butterflies, etc. Snakes were made from bits of skipping rope.
3. Glue the animals on to the background, then decorate lavishly with glued on pieces of fabric greenery, netting, raffia, creepers, ribbon, chiffon, etc., so that the animals are partially obscured.
4. Glue on to a frame a strip of rippled green material (see page 61) and add a few flowers cut from fabric.

Bethlehem Sunset

Materials:
Piece of white cotton cloth
Painting dyes in yellow, red and blue
Oddments of felt

Method:
1. Wet the cloth and then dye it by painting stripes of colour across. Start with blue at the top, then red, then yellow. Allow the colours to bleed together freely, making oranges and purples. Add water or extra colour here and there to blend in a pleasing way. Allow to dry.
2. Cut houses, hills and palm trees from felt and glue these on to the background.

For details of further Belair publications
please write to:
BELAIR PUBLICATIONS LIMITED
P.O. Box 12, TWICKENHAM, TW1 2QL, England

For sales and distribution (outside North America and South America)
FOLENS PUBLISHERS
Albert House, Apex Business Centre,
Boscombe Road, Dunstable, Bedfordshire, LU5 4RL
England

For sales and distribution in North America and South America
INCENTIVE PUBLICATIONS
3835 Cleghorn Avenue, Nashville, Tn 37215, U.S.A.

For sales and distribution in Australia
EDUCATIONAL SUPPLIES PTY LTD
8 Cross Street, Brookvale, N.S.W. 2100
Australia